## PART ONE     E♭ Alto Saxophone

# FIRST DIVISION BAND COURSE

# FIRST DIVISION BAND METHOD

### by FRED WEBER

**HELLO, Band Students:**

You are about to start an activity that should bring you much pleasure, fun, and happiness. As with all worthwhile things, a reasonable amount of effort and work, together with daily practice, will be necessary for success. We have tried in every way possible to make the work in this book enjoyable and challenging to you. At the same time it provides for the fine background in musical fundamentals so necessary to become a good player. Your success will depend to a large degree on the effort you put forth. Remember: The better player you become, the more fun you will have.

Best wishes in your new undertaking.

Sir
7̶
Au    D0877849    od

### Published for

| | |
|---|---|
| Conductor & Piano Accompaniment | E♭ Baritone Saxophone |
| Flute | B♭ Trumpet |
| B♭ Clarinet | Horn in F |
| E♭ Alto Clarinet | Trombone |
| B♭ Bass Clarinet | Baritone B.C. |
| Oboe | Baritone T.C. |
| Bassoon | Tuba |
| E♭ Alto Saxophone | Drums |
| B♭ Tenor Saxophone | Bells |

# ELEMENTARY FINGERING CHART

## How To Read The Chart

● - Indicates hole closed or keys to be pressed.

o - Indicates hole open.

When a number is given, refer to the picture of the Saxophone for additional key to be pressed.

When two ways to finger a note are given, the first way is the one most often used. The second fingering is for use in special situations.

When two notes are given together (F♯ and G♭) they are the same tone and, of course, played the same way.

Only those fingerings necessary in the Elementary Phase of Saxophone playing are given.

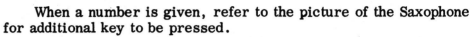

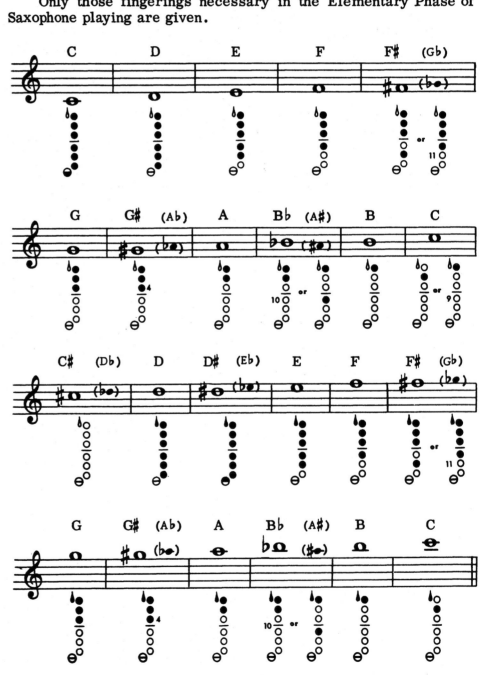

**To The Student:**

This Method Book is basic text for the FIRST DIVISION BAND COURSE series. To get the most enjoyment from your band activities and to ensure a good mastery of musical fundamentals, what you learn in the Method Book should be applied to the playing of solos, ensembles, and full band pieces as your skill increases.

On various pages in this Method Book, supplementary material is suggested, specially written for your playing ability. It is strongly recommended that these numbers be prepared as the various pages are reached.

## MATERIAL CORRELATED WITH THE FIRST DIVISION BAND METHOD, PART ONE:

### Solos for E♭ Alto Saxophone

TIME FOR SOLOS! BOOK ONE

Correlated to
Method pages:

FOX YOU STOLE
THE GOOSE . . . . . . . . . . . .German Folk Song . . . . . . . . . . . . . . . . 15
                                 arr. Sigurd Rascher

FROM HEAVEN HIGH . . . . .Michael Praetorius . . . . . . . . . . . . . . . . 15
                                 arr. Sigurd Rascher

CONCERT IN THE FOREST . . .Paul Baumann . . . . . . . . . . . . . . . . . . . 20
                                 arr. Sigurd Rascher

DRINK TO ME
ONLY WITH THINE EYES . . . .Old English Air . . . . . . . . . . . . . . . . . . 20
                                 arr. Sigurd Rascher

MINUET . . . . . . . . . . . . . .J. Fox . . . . . . . . . . . . . . . . . . . . . . . . . 24
                                 arr. Sigurd Rascher

A QUEMPAS TUNE . . . . . . . .Traditional . . . . . . . . . . . . . . . . . . . . . . 24
                                 arr. Sigurd Rascher

*(Some solos may also be available separately)*

### Technic
FUN WITH
FUNDAMENTALS . . . . . . . . .Bill Laas & Fred Weber . . . . . . . . Part 1 & 2

### Concert Band Books
OUR FIRST CONCERT ▪ AWAY WE GO ▪ PLAY AWAY ▪ CENTER STAGE

### Concert Band Pieces
FDB9901 . . . .BIG BASS BOOGIE . . . . . . . . . . . . . . . . . . . James D. Ployhar
FDB9902 . . . .MEXICANA . . . . . . . . . . . . . . . . . . . . . . . . . . arr. Frank Erickson
FDB9903 . . . .OVERTURE FOR YOUTH . . . . . . . . . . . . . . . . . Eric Osterling
FDB9904 . . . . . .SOMEBODY'S KNOCKING AT YOUR DOOR . . arr. James D. Ployhar
FDB9905 . . . .WILLIAM TELL (Featuring the Trumpet Section) . . . Michael Story
FDB9906 . . . .KRAZY KLOCK II . . . . . . . . . . . . . . . . . . . . . . . James D. Ployhar

# Know Your Instrument

## How To Assemble Your Instrument:

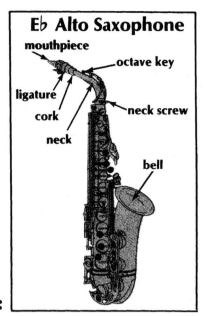

**E♭ Alto Saxophone**

1. Gently soak the reed in your mouth.

2. Place the NECK STRAP around your neck.

3. Hook the saxophone to the neck strap and remove the plug.

4. Place the NECK into the top of the instrument. DO NOT bend the octave key or octave key lever.

5. Tighten the NECK SCREW.

6. Now, hold the saxophone at the neck and gently twist the MOUTHPIECE onto the cork so that approximately half the cork is covered.

7. Align the flat side of the mouthpiece with the OCTAVE KEY.

## How To Place The Reed On The Mouthpiece:

1. Place the LIGATURE on the mouthpiece so that the ligature screws are on the flat side of the mouthpiece.

2. While pushing up the ligature with the thumb of one hand gently slide the reed under the ligature with the other hand. The flat side of the reed should be against the flat side of the mouthpiece.

3. Center the reed on the mouthpiece and have the tip of the reed even with the tip of the mouthpiece, or just slightly below the tip. At most there should be just a thin line of black showing as you hold the reed and mouthpiece at eye level.

4. Tighten the ligature until it is firm, but do not make it extremely tight.

## How To Hold Your Instrument:

1. Place the saxophone on the RIGHT side of your RIGHT leg.

2. Let the weight of the saxophone rest on the neck strap. DO NOT support the weight of the saxophone with your right thumb.

3. Place your RIGHT THUMB under the right thumb rest. Center your thumb at a point between the tip of the thumb and first knuckle.

4. Place your LEFT THUMB diagonally on the left thumb rest. You should be able to ROLL your left thumb onto the octave key.

5. Place the fleshy part of your fingers on the keys while maintaining a natural curve to your fingers.

Correct Position

Incorrect Position

These photos show you the proper way to hold the alto saxophone.

# GETTING STARTED

Study the pictures on Page 4 for the proper playing position. Check carefully the correct position of the mouth, hands, and fingers. You will need the help of your teacher to learn the proper way to produce a tone on the Saxophone. In preparing for our first lesson on the next page, it will be helpful to follow the preparatory steps given below.

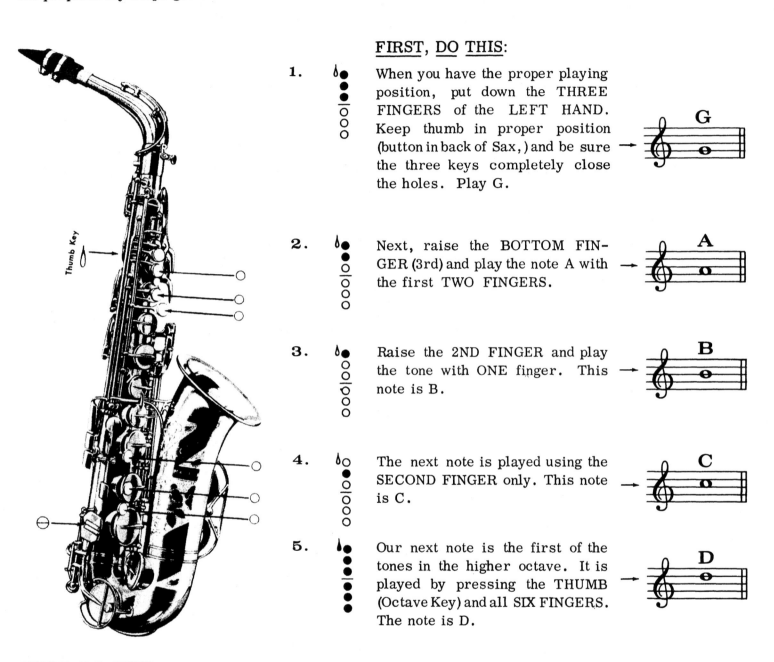

## FIRST, DO THIS:

1. When you have the proper playing position, put down the THREE FINGERS of the LEFT HAND. Keep thumb in proper position (button in back of Sax,) and be sure the three keys completely close the holes. Play G.

2. Next, raise the BOTTOM FINGER (3rd) and play the note A with the first TWO FINGERS.

3. Raise the 2ND FINGER and play the tone with ONE finger. This note is B.

4. The next note is played using the SECOND FINGER only. This note is C.

5. Our next note is the first of the tones in the higher octave. It is played by pressing the THUMB (Octave Key) and all SIX FINGERS. The note is D.

## NEXT, DO THIS:

Practice playing the notes below, in the order given:

### Going Up

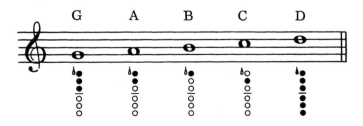

### Going Down

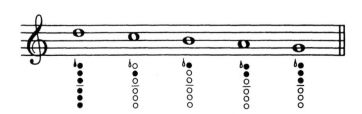

F.D.L.9

# Reading Music

You should know these things before we start to play.

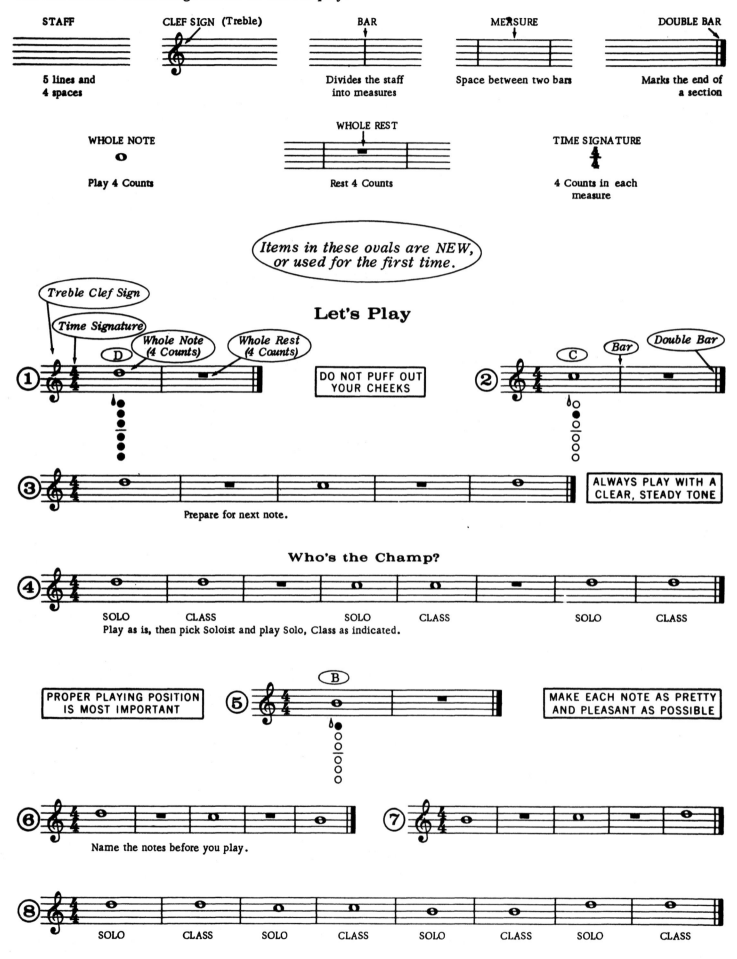

**STAFF** — 5 lines and 4 spaces

**CLEF SIGN (Treble)**

**BAR** — Divides the staff into measures

**MEASURE** — Space between two bars

**DOUBLE BAR** — Marks the end of a section

**WHOLE NOTE** — Play 4 Counts

**WHOLE REST** — Rest 4 Counts

**TIME SIGNATURE** — 4 Counts in each measure

*Items in these ovals are NEW, or used for the first time.*

## Let's Play

*Treble Clef Sign*
*Time Signature*
*Whole Note (4 Counts)*
*Whole Rest (4 Counts)*
D

DO NOT PUFF OUT YOUR CHEEKS

C *Bar* *Double Bar*

Prepare for next note.

ALWAYS PLAY WITH A CLEAR, STEADY TONE

### Who's the Champ?

SOLO  CLASS  SOLO  CLASS  SOLO  CLASS

Play as is, then pick Soloist and play Solo, Class as indicated.

PROPER PLAYING POSITION IS MOST IMPORTANT

B

MAKE EACH NOTE AS PRETTY AND PLEASANT AS POSSIBLE

Name the notes before you play.

SOLO  CLASS  SOLO  CLASS  SOLO  CLASS  SOLO  CLASS

For the first few pages name and finger the notes before you play each line.

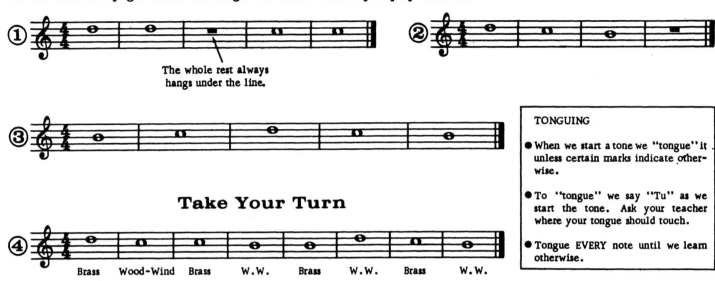

The whole rest always
hangs under the line.

### TONGUING

● When we start a tone we "tongue" it unless certain marks indicate otherwise.

● To "tongue" we say "Tu" as we start the tone. Ask your teacher where your tongue should touch.

● Tongue EVERY note until we learn otherwise.

## Take Your Turn

Brass    Wood-Wind    Brass    W.W.    Brass    W.W.    Brass    W.W.

## Quarter Notes and Rests

TONGUE EVERY NOTE

In this book there will be many times when two lines can be played together. This will be indicated by a broken vertical line joining them. Always learn each line separately first. The class should then be divided and the lines played together.

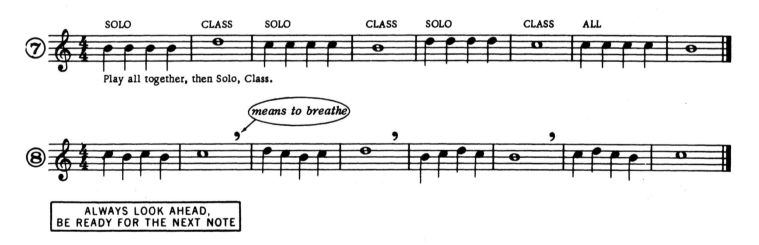

SOLO    CLASS    SOLO    CLASS    SOLO    CLASS    ALL

Play all together, then Solo, Class.

means to breathe

ALWAYS LOOK AHEAD,
BE READY FOR THE NEXT NOTE

## SAXOPHONE EXTRA

### New Notes

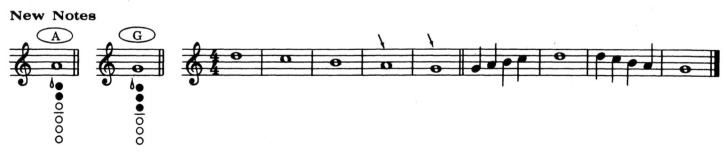

8

### A very important story

As a beginner the most important thing is the development of careful playing habits. Always be sure of these things:

1. Proper position - lips, hands, fingers, posture, etc.
2. Always get a pretty and pleasant tone with no wavers.
3. Tongue all notes correctly.
4. Blow plenty of AIR through the horn.
5. Always LISTEN carefully.

**New Note**

*Breathe*

## Harmony*

*Dotted Half Note (3 Counts)*

*Repeat Dots*

Always count steady.

*See Note below ⑥ on Page 7.

## Mary's Little Lamb

## Half Notes and Rests

*Half Note (2 Counts)* *Half Rest (2 Counts)*

TONGUE EVERY NOTE

Count ① ② ③ ④ Half Rest always sets on top of the line.

Count ① ② ③ ④

ALWAYS LOOK AHEAD

## Holiday In Paris (Duet)

*See Note below ⑥ on Page 7.

### Saxophone Extra

\* HARMONY - Two or more Tones played at the same time that have a pleasing sound.

## Solo Boy

## Counting Fun

## New Notes

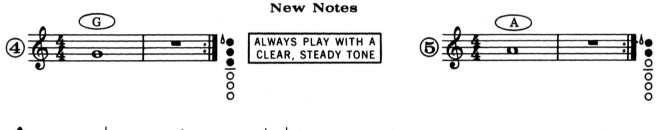

ALWAYS PLAY WITH A CLEAR, STEADY TONE

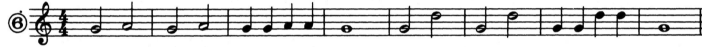

## Here's That Tune Again

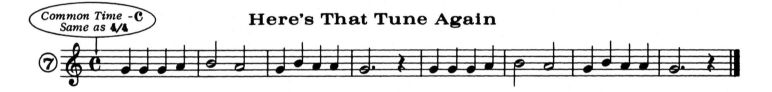

## The Two Tune Duet

Learn each line separately, then divide class and play together.

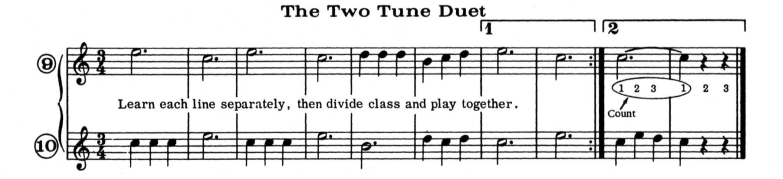

Put the following on the Staff:

| Whole Note | Flat | Quarter Note | A Time Signature | Quarter Rest | Half Note | Half Rest | Tie Two Notes |
|---|---|---|---|---|---|---|---|

## Comparing C and ¢ Time

¢ { *Means 2 Counts in each measure and ♩ gets ONE Count.*

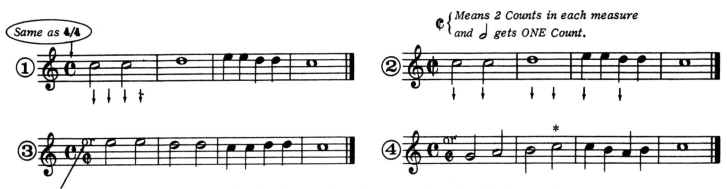

This means the line may be played either in **C** or **¢** time. Practice the line in **C** time until you can play it well, then play the notes <u>at</u> <u>the</u> <u>same</u> <u>speed</u> but TAP in **¢** time. The notes will sound the same, only the TAPPING will be different.

## Some Folks Do

## Band Chords

**In Harmony**

Part of class can play the above part while others play the chords.

## Counting Fun

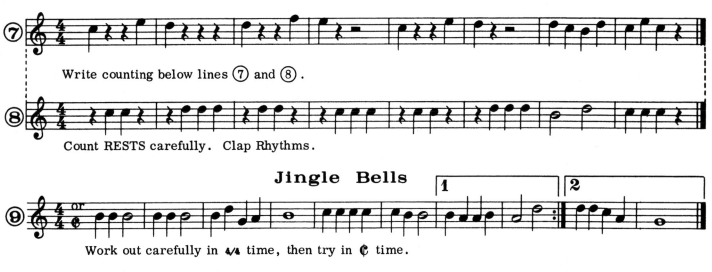

Write counting below lines ⑦ and ⑧.

Count RESTS carefully. Clap Rhythms.

## Jingle Bells

Work out carefully in **4/4** time, then try in **¢** time.

## The Tuneful Tooters (Duet)

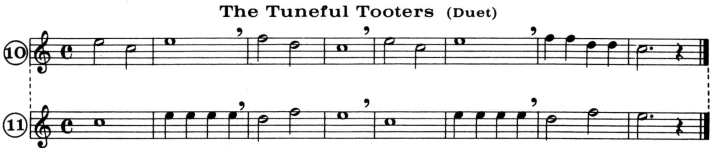

\* Ask your instructor about another way of fingering C when it is between 2 B's.

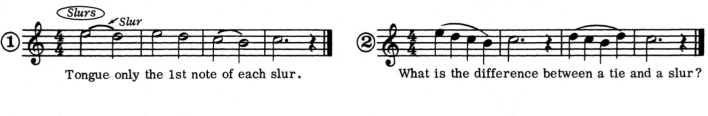

Tongue only the 1st note of each slur.

What is the difference between a tie and a slur?

1ST SOLOIST          2ND SOLOIST          3RD SOLOIST          ALL
ALL play on Repeat

## A Musical Game

Different instruments play the various notes of the Tune below. If everyone plays their note on the correct count you can easily name the tune. Who will be the first to name this tune?

**Group 3**

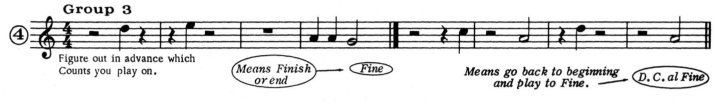

Figure out in advance which
Counts you play on.

*Means Finish or end* → *Fine*

*Means go back to beginning and play to Fine.* → *D. C. al Fine*

## London's Crazy Bridge

**Counting Fun**

Work out carefully, then try for speed.

*Hold each note as long as possible*

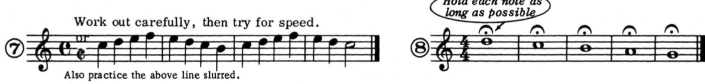

Also practice the above line slurred.

## The Two Tune March

*2 Counts in each measure*

**Tune II**

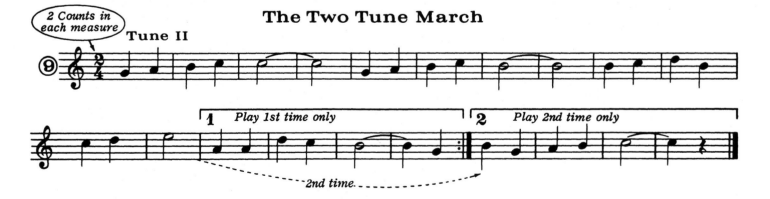

|1 *Play 1st time only*      |2 *Play 2nd time only*

*2nd time*

## Scale Fun (Review of Notes Learned)

**Saxophone Extra**

Work out carefully, then try for speed.

14

New Notes

New Notes

* KEY SIGNATURE: every F is played F♯ (See note below.)

To remind you

**Scale Fun**

Apply these patterns to each tone of the Scale above.

To remind you the note is F♯

**The Old Gray Goose**

Practice both octaves.

**Jumpin' Jack**

Pick-up Note: (Ask your teacher to explain.)

**A-Tiskit A-Taskit**

Count 4 1 etc.

**Crazy Counting**

Count 4 1 etc.
Write Counting under notes, then Play.

LISTEN CAREFULLY

**Chords**

**Nip And Tuck** (Duet)

* The sharps (or flats) at the beginning of a piece are called "Key Signature". When there is one sharp it is always F♯. When there are two sharps, they are always F♯ and C♯ and it means that every F and C is played F♯ and C♯ throughout the entire piece. We use the key signature so it won't be necessary to use a sharp (or flat) before each note.

## OUR FIRST SOLO

## I Love You Truly

You are now ready to play the first two solos from the book TIME FOR SOLOS! BOOK ONE. They were specially written for your playing ability at this time. It will be fun to get this book for your instrument and learn these solos.

16

New Notes

* LEGER LINES: Many times we use notes that go above or below the staff. We provide for these notes by adding short lines called Leger Lines. By placing notes on these lines, or the spaces between them, we are able to go above or below the Staff.

You are now ready to play a concert from your first full band book called OUR FIRST CONCERT. It was written by some of the country's finest band composers and arrangers.

### Dancing Girl

### Mr. F♯ and Mr. F

### Skips

The Top Tones below make a familiar tune. What is it?

*To remind you*

### Round

### Think! Look! And Listen! (Choral)

### Army Song

*Pick-up Notes - Why?*

MELODY

*Counter Melody* - a secondary melody

The Letters in the boxes below spell out a tune.
Write the notes on the staff. Play the tune. What is it? (Name)_____
(Use quarter notes and only notes you have learned in this book.)

| C | C | D | E | C | E | D | B | C | C | D | E | C | B | C | C | D | E | F | E | D | C | B | G | A | B | C | C |

**Featuring Mr. Clarinet**

**The Mouse And The Click**

**What's My Name?**

**Hear That German Band**

**The Carnival Of Venice**

* Chromatic means progressing by Half-Steps.

F.D.L.9

## Little Waltz

## Scale Duet

**The Victors**

Allegro - Fast

**Saxophone Extra**

*When going from B to C and back we use an alternate fingering for C.
Use this fingering for C (add Octave Key for high Octave).
(See Saxophone Extra on Page 22).

You are now ready to play the third and fourth solos from the book TIME FOR SOLOS! BOOK ONE. We know you will like playing them.

# Three ways to count Old MacDonald

# There's A Hole In The Bucket

## Billy Boy

## This Old Man

## Round And Round We Go

## Crazy Counting

## Skip To M' Lou

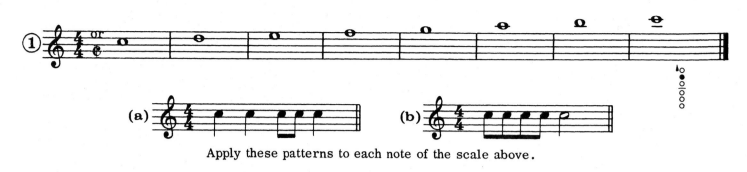

Apply these patterns to each note of the scale above.

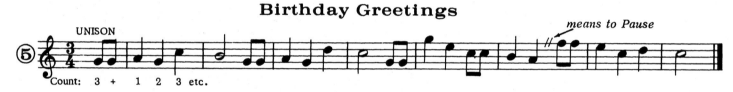

## The Blue Tail Fly

## Birthday Greetings

## Three Tunes

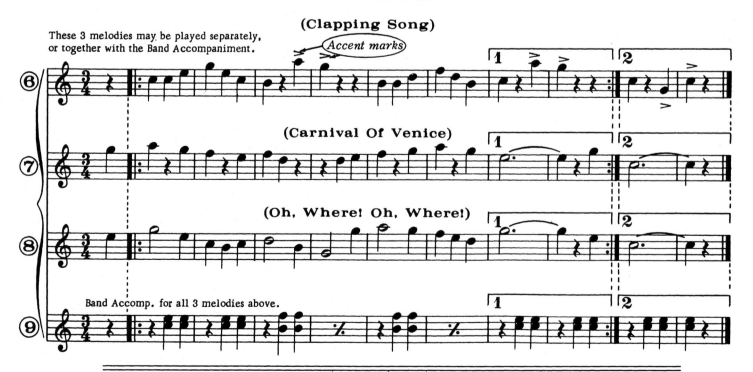

The fifth and sixth solos of TIME FOR SOLOS! BOOK ONE should be learned at this time. These solos can be used for Solo Festival participation.

## Play Tunes

The pieces on this page are for extra practice and recreation. You may try them whenever you feel you are able to play them. All instruments may play together except E♭ Mellophone, Horn in F, Oboe, and Tenor Saxophone. Piano Accomp. in Conductor's Book.

### Home On The Range

### We Wish You A Merry Christmas

### I'm Called Little Buttercup

### When The Saints Go Marching In

### Red River Valley

### Taps

F.D.L.9

# Review and Rating

(For <u>like</u> Instruments only)

**Notes**

**Counting**

**Time Signature**

**Key Signature**

**Slurring**

**Tone**

*Slowly*    *Breathe*

Very smooth and Songlike

**Etude**

8 – Play the C Scale up and down from Memory, slowly, 1 count on each note.

9 – Solo

10 – Ensembles

|  | Points |  | Points |
|---|---|---|---|
| (Perfect is 10) |  | (Perfect is 10) |  |
| 1 - Notes |  | 6 - Tone |  |
| 2 - Counting |  | 7 - Etude |  |
| 3 - Time Signatures |  | 8 - Scale |  |
| 4 - Key Signatures |  | 9 - SOLO |  |
| 5 - Slurring |  | 10 - ENSEMBLES |  |
|  |  |  |  |
| TOTAL POINTS ———————— |  |  |  |

The teacher may use this Review and Rating page as he or she chooses. Each line may be played individually and rated by the teacher, or the page can be used as a review lesson. It may be the basis for awarding a certificate or diploma, or it may be used as a final rating for a report card or as a final record of accomplishment on completion of this book. Every item is rated on the basis of 10 possible points. The solo and ensemble categories should be rated on how well you performed any solos or ensembles during the year.

# BAND CONCERT

## Away We Go

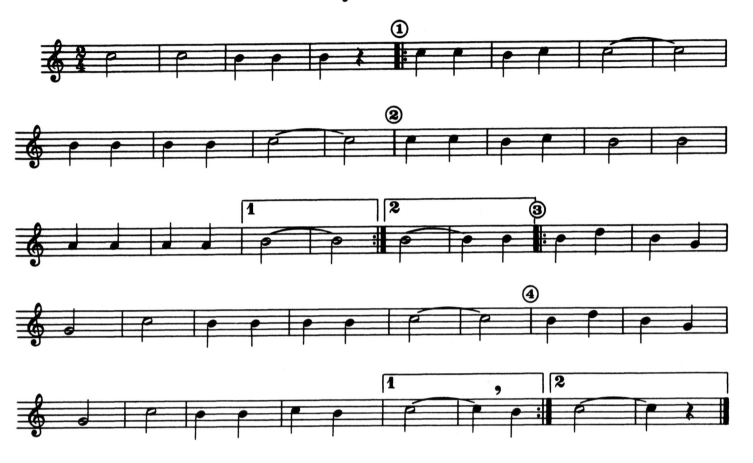

## Two Famous Waltz Melodies

# Musical Signs and Terms
### (See page 6 for 1st elements of music)

| Notes | and | Rests |
|---|---|---|
| o — | Whole | — |
| ♩ — | Half | — |
| ♩. — | Dotted Half | — |
| ♩ — | Quarter | — ♪ |
| ♪ — | Eighth | — 𝄾 |

## Time Signatures

| | |
|---|---|
| **4/4** | 4 beats in each measure. <br> each ♩ note gets one beat. |
| **C** | Common Time - same as 4/4 |
| **3/4** | 3 beats in each measure. <br> each ♩ note gets one beat. |
| **2/4** | 2 beats in each measure. <br> each ♩ note gets one beat. |
| **¢** | 2 beats in each measure. <br> each ♩ note gets one beat. |

♭ —— Flat - Lowers a tone a ½ step.

♯ —— Sharp - Raises a tone a ½ step.

♮ —— Natural - Indicates that the note is not to be sharped or flatted. It cancels the effect of a sharp or flat.

⁹ —— Breath Mark

Repeat Dots - Repeat entire section.

1st and 2nd endings. Play 1st ending the first time then repeat strain and play 2nd ending.

o ♩ Tie - Combines two or more tones.

Chord - A combination of different tones that is pleasant to the ear.

*Fine* - Finish - The end.

*D.C. al Fine* - Go back to the beginning and play until you come to Fine.

Scale - A series of notes that follow a definite pattern of half steps and whole steps.

•/. - Repeat the preceding measure.

Waltz - A type of dance in 3/4 time.

Accompaniment - A part that supports the melody but is subordinate to it.

## Home Practice Record

| WEEK | MON. | TUES. | WED. | THURS. | FRI. | SAT. | PARENT'S SIGNATURE | WEEK | MON. | TUES. | WED. | THURS. | FRI. | SAT. | PARENT'S SIGNATURE |
|---|---|---|---|---|---|---|---|---|---|---|---|---|---|---|---|
| 1 | | | | | | | | 19 | | | | | | | |
| 2 | | | | | | | | 20 | | | | | | | |
| 3 | | | | | | | | 21 | | | | | | | |
| 4 | | | | | | | | 22 | | | | | | | |
| 5 | | | | | | | | 23 | | | | | | | |
| 6 | | | | | | | | 24 | | | | | | | |
| 7 | | | | | | | | 25 | | | | | | | |
| 8 | | | | | | | | 26 | | | | | | | |
| 9 | | | | | | | | 27 | | | | | | | |
| 10 | | | | | | | | 28 | | | | | | | |
| 11 | | | | | | | | 29 | | | | | | | |
| 12 | | | | | | | | 30 | | | | | | | |
| 13 | | | | | | | | 31 | | | | | | | |
| 14 | | | | | | | | 32 | | | | | | | |
| 15 | | | | | | | | 33 | | | | | | | |
| 16 | | | | | | | | 34 | | | | | | | |
| 17 | | | | | | | | 35 | | | | | | | |
| 18 | | | | | | | | 36 | | | | | | | |